THE LAST OF AZIZI

Pull over this night, a sleep, I'm not seeking!

For, to His nightshade eyes, no more, İ am seeing.

No desire left in me for dreaming,

For in dreams with you, I am not meeting!

Let the Sun be black, the sky turn dark!

For, without You bright, my eyes abandoned seeing!

Let the stars fall apart, clearing the path.

For to you again, it is not leading!

Let my garden barren again.

Without you my heart's not springing.

And let my heart be torn apart!

For You in it, I am not sighting.

Let me blind, my eyes loose its sight!

For to You, they aren't sighting.

1

Isabel Ayesha Khalid

Let me crawl on ground, with no might!

For to You, I am not striding.

Let my tongue cease to talk,

For to gain You, it is not fighting!

Let my pen cease to write,

For my name with You, it isn't writing!

And let my breath cease for death,

Without You, there is no living!

There was once an Azizi, I guess?

Today for good, to her I'm burying!

From the most beloved of thee, my Love,

Today, an unknown name, I'm becoming!

Call me not Azizi ever,

Today I'm gone, I am never returning!

Isabel Ayesha Khalid

(1)

With ink of dry lakes, let me write Your presence in my name

With eyes that cry in aches, let me sight Your absence fame

Like the undressed widow of love, let me die in Your carless shame

Like the candle burning its love, let me ash before I stain

The stain of being called the forsaken,

Save me, before I lose Your name

And when I do so, I wander in wonder

Let the setting Sun, the divided moon remind me of You

Let the glance of desert's flower, hint me Your clue

3

Isabel Ayesha Khalid

And when I lose, in the vague of color's hue

Remind me of You, through my heart's smoke,
burning through!

Isabel Ayesha Khalid

(2)

In between Your arms, my eyes do cry

Stretched between memory alarms, my heart does
die

In this full bloomed world, in my love's barren isle

A queer flower bloom, I, in spring who does sigh

Under my tear's stream, come let's meet by

Let me soar in Your song's melody, above so high

And let me adorn the flowers with dew

So, when You return, You may find me due,

To the rainy clouds and bloody rose's clue

Call out my name, trace Your echo's trail

And if You won't find me, perhaps You may fail

Then go, visit the cemetery, a dead's jail

And if I'm not there, lest You fail,

Isabel Ayesha Khalid

The Last of Azizi

Go visit the skies and birds from earth who bail

Let them sing a song, and built a trail

And if I'm not there, lest You fail,

Seeking me out, with a pain You cannot bare

Search in Your heart, call Azizi, I'm there

Hiding from You, so to me with other's, You do not share

Veiling, testing how much You care

Isabel Ayesha Khalid

(3)

Out of my flesh, I'll sew a cloak for You

From my soul, I'll bloom a rose so true

*To keep You warm, I'll present my heart's burning
stew*

Tisk, You will leave! And move with another crew!

And if ever You cry, or loose in autumn's hue

*Pluck out my petal, sniff deep in my fragrance for
You*

*Yet again You shall leave, with another, You may
crew*

In the middle of desert, if You loose

*Smile at other, out of anguish, spring's of water I'll
flow*

Quench Your thirst, with another walk through

7

Isabel Ayesha Khalid

Causing You relief, would end my rue

Someday, when my all petals are plucked

I will remain, the only perfume, burning in You

The only essence left in Muhammed's heart

An ashed heart, who no one knew

Azizi awaits for this day to come

Till then she's a love-struck slew

Isabel Ayesha Khalid

(4)

Turn away from me, O my honey taste flower!

Turn away, before I consider You mine, my lovely devour!

For You'll be plucked; like a lonely nightingale, I shall wander in glower

For I know, the moment You're mine, Your honey would turn so sour,

Ripping my heart, forsaking me in spring's hour

Let me not taste Your lips, let me hide in cower

Turn away Your face, before in love, my heart lose power

Hide Your sway, lest I'm swept in love of our

Shove me away, before Sun vanishes in bower

But what can I do? For in love with You, I've fallen

9

Isabel Ayesha Khalid

Turn away I can't say; I'll die, if You come any
closer

Poor Azizi love-struck now homeless,

Gave her heart, to a Seth-holder, her devourer

Who shall follow my heart, in the city of mediocre

Move Naimi! This is not Your home

Hiding from love, then tracing it

There's no abode for such a rover!

Isabel Ayesha Khalid

Even if You turn away, from me Your face

You are in me! İ know, it is a phase

No matter how much You tend to test

Till the end, only You'll remain my one craze

Now come and do help me O grace!

Before Azizi and all You knew, they do erase

11

Isabel Ayesha Khalid

Silent O Mouzin! Stay silent my plea

Before tearing body, my Soul does flee

Towards it's Beloved, for union to be

Silent O Mouzin! Be silent my plea!

Do You desire, my death to see?

Or seeing my liver and heart to bleed

You call Muhammad and pay no heed?

The name which tears my soul

And ceases my sins to grow

You can't imagine, what he means to me

The only Spring to, a pity bee

The only cure, to a thirsting sea

To only sight, of a sightless me

The only fruit, of a fruitless tree

12

Isabel Ayesha Khalid

And You plot on messing, how ruthless of thee

Another ditch, I cannot bare

Don't pretend that way, he may be near

Do You test a Lover, with her one so Dear

Casting a fish of water, and making her glare

To put her in anguishes quenchless flare

Call not His name, for He isn't near

Don't tempt Azizi, with unattended call, to me do hear!

Isabel Ayesha Khalid

(7)

Upon me, Your first sight,

Like first ray of Sun so bright,

Like first rain in summer's blight,

Like first glide of bird's flight

Upon my hands Your feeble clutch,

Like water's, to thirsty desert a touch,

Like lips of snow against mount so drudge,

Like moon melting in love's grudge,

A grudge to remain a miss-judge,

For elevation You chose a kludge

Failing again and failure I come

For You every time, a disappointment, I become

Yet You love me! Yet, how come?

14

Isabel Ayesha Khalid

Azizi ashamed of seeing You, dying in glum

Missing Muhammad, yet can't say come!

Isabel Ayesha Khalid

(8)

Smelled many a flower,

Of You, found scent in none

Roamed around with scorn and glower,

Seems, not caring of me, You've begun

Spend my nights in cower,

Why, for sheltering me, You're not here?

How long You're to take? Now please come near

İ saw the Moon shining, undivided,

Causing my tears to stream, missing You, my dear

For this Moon is forsaken, sicken, in absence of Sun

Azizi left no more azizi perhaps,

Kill her, instead of keeping in fear

16

Isabel Ayesha Khalid

(9)

My people are dying O Lord save me!

Their souls are defying; evils play win

You're here end, yet they're crying?

Your such presence has become my grim

Azizi is there a Lord to look out for You?

Perhaps thinking this, was my only sin

A silent show maker is my Beloved King

17

Isabel Ayesha Khalid

(10)

A touch softer than snow, warmer than summer's
blow

A floating floe, denser than mountain's dough

Gentle than birds feather so new, with power of
revolution so true

Found myself in the crew of Who, the Holy Spirit
within grew

My heart was heavy, the world to me withdrew

Then appeared the One, with a style so new

In warmth of His words my pain flew, leaving in me
grief not even a few

In the Dusk of His hair the dust of my deeds blew

In blush of His eve smile, my faith grew

Now how from Him, I may depart? Come see He's
my heart

18

*A Spring to this decayed rose He became, saving
her from Autumn's drought*

*Who shall Azizi recognize after Him? Beloved's
touch is all I fraught*

19

(11)

Two butterflies in the garden flying, claiming,

'We are in love!'

The same flower attracts them, they're thinking,

We are in love

A voice echos to them from the wilderness,

Fly away from this hell, there's nothing,

Like, we are in love

Their hearts were united, unaware of destinies cruelness

Soon arrived Autumn, leaving them faded colorless

With time grew their familiarity and alas, strangeness

Somehow, crossed they all the seasons in a sweet bitterness

20

Isabel Ayesha Khalid

The more they grew near, it lessened their eagerness

Sick of one and other, butterflies are screaming,

Striking every thorn and begging,

Release us from this love

Even if You find Your reflection in one,

Pay heed to story of the butterflies above

Azizi! There is nothing existing like love.

Isabel Ayesha Khalid

(12)

A nightingale longs for spring to arrive

For, it's missing Beloved flower, and so deprive

Lays its nest in the middle of marshes

Day and night in hope, the flower may survive

Now that arrives Spring, in its full bloom

Before they could kiss, the nightingale stayed no more alive

A silent Seth-holder is the destiny, trust not

Don't fall in love, for it don't thrive

Even if true love to You does find, to it forget Azizi,

Beware, if fallen in love, You're destinies jive

22

Isabel Ayesha Khalid

Cold blooded in dry eyes

Heart's melted with no cries

Laughing a laugh, though in grief lies

Screaming within, but with no voice

A laughter I laugh, a laughter with no joy

A sober or senseless can't tell I,

A Paradise is Azizi, who's within hell lies

Isabel Ayesha Khalid

(13)

I bare stain of love, from my Love; no One, I can blame

Oh it has pain too much, I cannot shove; to whom shall I complain?

In fake smile I hide, in darks of night, I can't conceal my shame!

For it is in You, it came from You; it hurts, I called Your name!

24

Isabel Ayesha Khalid

(14)

To me what good, Your rosy lips?

If fail to kiss in the lofty spring

Upon my cheek a blush, if it cannot bring

A song of dew to me, if it cannot sing

To me what good, Your dazzling beauty

To my lightless eyes, if cannot bright

To my burdened heart, if cannot light

For my every tear, if cannot fight

To me what use, Your unfailing love

If cannot dissolve, in every tear

Like a selfless moth, in You when I burn,

What good to me, Your love so sheer

25

Isabel Ayesha Khalid

Like my heart if You do not tear

What kind of Love You offer to me

If death turns away, You're not in fear

When I walk away and You still stay?

What good to me is His love Azizi?

To You he sees, to Him, you cannot see!

Isabel Ayesha Khalid

(15)

Someone, kept İ, so, secretly

So that someone, I can't describe

Someone I, preferred as my spring, elusively

That someone, whom I can't prescribe

İnstead, appearing of Him, so deadly,

To my heart, autumn did swipe

Now I scream to that someone, not secretly,

With the tears of heart rip so bad

That someone got offended, so openly

That dragged, a scar so black

He considered my love the fruit, though,

For the spring my heart fought

27

Isabel Ayesha Khalid

That someone, so secretly dear, may frown,

Upon my screams so brown,

For they'll last till my heart does cry

Will they be healed in discreet, by that Someone of

my ?

28

(16)

How queer is it, between You and me

Stretched by time, yet in hearts nothing between

They call Your name, as You're here

Oh You won't come, You won't come for me

The place of Azizi with Muhammad only

He's with me, yet with me, I see no thee

29

(17)

My flowing tears, don't contrast my smile

Let me play a pretend, just for a while

In discreet, I am all yours my grief

I'll sail in tears of lonely isle

For You're not to see me cry

Nor are You to come by

Willing to leave without goodbye

My flowing tears don't contrast my smile

At least for a little while

Conceal my unfailing love for thee

Don't make hard this goodbye

Azizi is still waiting for thee

Isabel Ayesha Khalid

An innocent plea, consider of me

Maybe He stays, can't seeing me cry

31

(18)

In wild passion, I recklessly dive

From my heart a memory of You to drive

Oceans of tears, I shed in thrive

Suffocating within, finding You by

Seems what parts you from me, is Your new hive

Let me see You! Before I live, before I die

Hoping to see You, finally arrive

Like Dove in passion I whirl and jive

David, I became, David's Lord to me came

Yet, fate of loneliness became my sive

Upon hearing Your name, I do cry

Without Your name, I cannot survive

Isabel Ayesha Khalid

Causing such pain, what is Your shrive?

From Muhammad do You expect,

Leaving alone Azizi, in pain and deject?

For this promise, yet, did ever You strive?

Saving me to swim in tears to dive?

Isabel Ayesha Khalid

The Last of Azizi

Isabel Ayesha Khalid

(19)

Towards the Sun I sail, once again

In holding Your hands I fail, all in vein

In water, for I wrote Your name, it flowed with rain

Across the sky I got Your fame, alas the stars do not reign

Oh what could do I? Love's a losing game!

In my heart then, once again, I wrote Your name

Like the burning Sun, for You, I did flame

Yet again I lost to You! Oh what a shame!

My fragile heart was crushed, carrying Your name

My dawning Sun did set, in eve's cruel shame

I once again lost in this losing game

To the stars I begged again, map me to You

35

Isabel Ayesha Khalid

I fire kissed the lake, I steamed and flew

In heavens I reached Your doors, but who knew,

Upon the flowers I lived once, now You're it's dew

In anguish was left I, towards the world I took flight

He wasn't there, left He, leaving no clue

This is me, a desperate one remain I

Still in hope He'll come, a lovely pursue?

Isabel Ayesha Khalid

(20)

Like a butterfly laying lips on my flower

Day and night in its sweetness and sour

Like moon disappears in the breast of Sun

O how, you spend with me, every hour!

Yet, disappeared you, in the sun kissed eve

I followed you, like sun tracking sunflower

We kissed again, a kiss not sweet nor sour

I stood along, silent at the bay of glower.

Seeing you selling me away, in our love's tower

I sailed away, as you left without signaling however

Dry as desert stood I, in middle of springy auer

You melted away into another, as counter.

37

Isabel Ayesha Khalid

Expect me to stay Yours, and asked that all louder?

Azizi was forgotten by beloved, that hour

Rivers ran black and Sun never to be seen,

Soul of mine melted, my liver a red flower.

Isabel Ayesha Khalid

(21)

Wearing the veil of night

Hoping the Sun to sight

Who could sight Leyla,

But the eyes of Mejnun

With dry eyes, what a knight?

With fixed heart, with no fight?

39

Isabel Ayesha Khalid

(22)

When he revealed his glory

Kneeled all high and lowly

Stayed one neck straight, starting all quarry

Nothing could bent its neck so flinty

Who knew, what's behind it the story

While they bowed, in the eyes of Beloved she
drowned

O! Who could see the pain in her eyes?

The pain to see self from Beloved self apart

Kneel all kneelers! As for the accused Azizi

From the gaze of Beloved, will never be depart

One dive into the eyes of Beloved,

Cursed Azizi with eternity of tears dart

40

Isabel Ayesha Khalid

(23)

İn He I hide, in me hides He

Native in His heart stays me

Every reason to my pain and glee

Now, that became my every desire, Thee

Secure with You, without Him in storm

A rose adorned in countless thorn

Picked Azizi, the same scent

Who became her soul, her heart, the flesh was she

41

Isabel Ayesha Khalid

(24)

Gathered around me from all directs

Lovers with, for me much expects

To unite me with my One true Love

Arrived spring, in different dialects

Gushed around me cool breeze

To remind me, His sweet essence

Don't awake, O Eastern winds,

Go back, O western breeze,

Set down, O rising Sun

Don't bloom, my new spring flower

For, whomsoever, will go visit my One true Love

Will never return, and belong to Him

Isabel Ayesha Khalid

The Last of Azizi

For His eyes, the blanket of night

Hiding from me, my endless blight

His sight, than day bright

Providing to all, a seeing light

His blushing cheek more pleasant than eve

You'll visit him and belong to He

And forget to pay my greets

But that's not, bothering me

I firmly desire with Him to meet

For, He's the source of all my glee

Poor Azizi, can't stare at the One

Neither is forgetting Him an option,

The One, Who's become, her universe,

Even close than the blood in veins that run

43

Isabel Ayesha Khalid

(25)

Hear O people! Hear my nation!

For the voice, I've heard, is splendid indeed

A melody, so strange, that will bless You with hearing,

A hearing so great, that, deaf You from world

A fragrance so sweet, that may taste You bitter

A bitterness, so wired, making You sweet than sugar

Hear O people! Give ear, o nation of mine,

Like the wind passing by us, a need so essential

Before You suffocate, breathe, breathe, O my people of my!

Azizi, in wilderness, forgets what's the universe

This forgetfulness, made her the Universe

44

Isabel Ayesha Khalid

(26)

To sight the state of my drunken heart

Appeared bright Moon, from far apart,

Tearing the horizon, forming a crimson art

The Moon is now my lamp, the sky reflect,

My bleeding liver, my heart,

Even if I tend to seek ease of pain,

I know it's nor morale,

Pain is love's one art

45

Isabel Ayesha Khalid

(27)

After showing the face of ocean

The fish was shove away, into oblivion

This isn't my luck, but my love's doing

To leave a Moon, desperate of completion

İt bothers me not anymore, am I dead?

No! I'm the part of this delusion

The land You longed for never existed

İt was nothing, but a land of illusion

Snap out Azizi, Your tears worth more

Don't waste them upon, a mindless confusion

46

Isabel Ayesha Khalid

(28)

To sight the state of my drunken heart

Appeared bright Moon, from apart,

Tearing the horizon, forming a crimson art

The Moon is now my lamp, the sky reflect,

My bleeding liver, my heart,

Even if I tend to seek ease of pain

Hoping, praying to Beloved, everyday,

To lighten my pain, letting it heal

And burn not so much, that loses it's capacity to feel

But I'm not certain of what I pray

What is pain? And what is love without it?

Is it my love or sorrows that make me kneel

Poor Azizi, asks this question walking at heel

Is there a wound that could ever heal?

47

Isabel Ayesha Khalid

(29)

İ don't know, what You intend to say

But it doesn't, help me, cease my pain

Seems it's my love's only gain

To see my tears rain

İ can't see, what is waiting for me

But I feel, it's to stain me

With a stain of love, so sheer

Death awaits, isn't it so clear

İf death means to unite with You

Then wait not, swipe me in to

But I can't see You by the end

What can I do, neither fright nor fret?

Isabel Ayesha Khalid

İ don't know, what's waiting for me

Till it's You, all pain's I'll live

For You're my only life in me

Leave me not, a poor Azizi to be

49

Isabel Ayesha Khalid

(30)

From the meadow of meadows

Returned a Lamb, in mellow

From the herd to her, no one heard

From green pastures, she returned too Yellow

O Shepard! Hear to my cry

For Your Lamb, has fallen of the track

Except You to her, who could bring back?

For without You, in me, glee I lack

Now come to me, find me, and bring me back!

To the Meadow of Meadows,

Where, the Sun never sets,

The running river, never let's,

Isabel Ayesha Khalid

The Last of Azizi

The flow of, love to, cease in it

Return me, to the place, where

The Sun and Moon are together,

Even the cries sound, as laughter

Come to me! My heart waits, for slaughter,

I'm Your Child, at Bani Ismaili's alter,

Let me lay my heart, for after,

You, no laugh, seems to me laughter

All my dreams, are now shatter

So, find me my Shepherd!

Your Lamb is, ready for slaughter

Azizi's heart must stain the alter

The alter of love awaits, come closer

51

Isabel Ayesha Khalid

(31)

When You're here, in my heart

What's then, keeping us apart?

When I've considered You, my part

Then why is departure, Your only art?

İ know, You can't see me crying

Then why is, in absence of Muhammad,

His dearest, Azizi dying?

Can the Gardner, see, his dear flower, draying...?

Isabel Ayesha Khalid

(32)

The shadows, of darkness, are ended

A fellow, of enlightenment, I'm appointment

İn the Love, of Adonai, I'm blended

His name, Yahweh; to foes, has offended

To every inch of fear in me, he's evacuated

İn shadows of darkness; to me, He has enlightened

From kingdom of Devil, to me, He did deliver

At table of poison, with good, to me, He did fed

İn company, of most Beloved, to me, He did raise

Then in the whole universe, Azizi, to me, He did praise.

53

Isabel Ayesha Khalid

(34)

İn the middle of a thirsty desert

A flower, bloomed I

Seeing all around me, the desert dirt

Travelers left me, and I gloomed

Then once it rained in the desert

But I was still thirsty, all fancied me doomed

Then a rose appeared, near me lilies grew

And I rejoiced, henceforth, in my crew

Plucking the plucks of plant, did a shepherd so new

That plucking plucked, the strings of my heart

Soon of that Shepard, I became a part

Now once again, in the middle of thirsty desert I
thirst,

54

Isabel Ayesha Khalid

A longing flower is Azizi, missing her Shepard who
drew

Her, near herself, She misses Him true

55

(35)

Talking leap of faith

When hollow was fate

Walking to destination in gladness

When path was blanketed in darkness

Reached for the boat that day

When it sure, left it's bey

Poor Azizi in her wrecked tray

Tangled in her actions frey

Wondering, to wander to where?

Isabel Ayesha Khalid

(36)

From east to west

Your love in all does manifest

An endless treasure, confined in no chest

Fully drenched in, yet, I in a quest

Turning into a sea, Alas! An endless thirst

Azizi, neither to the east nor the west

But in Your heart, is your Lover's chest

57

(37)

Leave me not Beloved! I'm begging You, leave not me, alone!

Stay so close! I'm dying, be gone, not so long!

My breath without You, I'm not breathing, don't break my song!

Without You I need no voice, can't You see, only to You, I belong!

If You desire to leave, kill me first! Accept my plea I'm begging!

Leave me not Beloved! I'm begging You, leave not me, alone!

Your Azizi I'll stay, without You my breath, I'll suffocate to death for long, leave me not!

58

Isabel Ayesha Khalid

Like the contrast between day and night

Like the contrast between You and I

İn the vacuum of that love I fly

Like the Moon, hiding its Sun so shy

So do İ, so no one steals You by

Between the contrast of day and night

İn You my Dawn I hide, fighting Your absence
blight

Between the contrast of You and me

For both are Thee; to You I sight

59

(39)

By the One, with whom rests my soul

This is tyranny, an ache above all

Shoving a Fish out of its home

Again and again teasing, water is shown

By the One, with whom rests my soul!

I will complain of You, by means of all

My Muhammad is gone, now am I Your awl?

Before Almighty, I'll sue Your aching brawl

Whom shall this Azizi blame after all

Are the ones teasing me, causing my countless tears to fall?

Or Beloved Muhammad, the One,

Leaving in departure, a lonely me to crawl

What You're to say my Love, come say it all

For Azizi won't pay heed to another's call

Isabel Ayesha Khalid

Return back O messengers of Muhammad, to You
I'm dall

Only upon voice of Beloved, my head shall fall

If You intend to leave me Muhammad my Love

Over my dead body, You have to brawl!

For except You another, Azizi is none to recall!

Isabel Ayesha Khalid

(40)

You say, 'see the all as reflection of mine'

İt's a deflection, for in whole, You don't stand by

You're the only image in my eyes that lye

But again! İt's an image not You my Alley

Azizi is strapped in an endless misery of love

You're the cure, although You're love causes me die

62

Isabel Ayesha Khalid

(41)

Raised a Nightingale me,

İn immense of love to Spring, thee

· O how occupied in You, I find She

Unless told You, there's no Spring to be

Whole life, built İ nest of love so sheer

A rainbow the Sun gifted, but who's to see

İn nightshade built a boat, so may travel to glee

Lend İ did my tears to clouds to rain a sea

Then to protect You from drops, became I the tree

For Your hair to flutter, the pleasant air became me

To Your head to spin, the melody I became, You
sing

So may not fall You, Your wings I'm being

Now tells me the universe, You're not mine to be

My nest, the sun, the boat and tree

63

Isabel Ayesha Khalid

The Last of Azizi

The air for Your fluttering hair, now how I'll see

The stream for You glee, became my tears

The tree for Your shade, burnt me in fears

For whom I was born, no more there he stay

So is Azizi nothing but an endless tears bay

A meaningless clay meant to fray

Without her Soul, in Muhammed that stay

Isabel Ayesha Khalid

(42)

The One with praise so Great, to me is raising

Above heavens and Earth, to me is keeping

Between Me and Him, no vacuum he's leaving

Each and every of him creation, in me is breathing

For I'm the breath, Of the most High the Living

To me confines none but longings of him are killing

Abiding in him for glee, in him hiding to see

*What is and what was and what's that's becoming
me*

*Azizi the Soul of eternal; although eternity in me
does flee*

*When You're not around, in me I'm tracing, funeral,
see*

65

Isabel Ayesha Khalid

(43)

A tree of life is being cut

Although it's pain it's still and stud

Due to the roots connecting to it's one true love

It's not falling, it sustains but

It worries not its head to lose

For its life is in love, connected to root

66

(44)

If You intend to see my tears following, I'll flood
them for You

If You desire my heart breaking, I'll crush it, so true

So tell me what You desire from Azizi, what's new?

For Your turning away can't be bared, her soul
would blew!

67

(45)

Left am I, so speechless; for me, no words to say

Bereft am I, so boundless; all stirred in sorrows bay

Cleft me, Your Moon, You heartless; in a single sway

Theft my heart being soundless; leaving there no bey

Left am I, in loneliness; vanished from my hefte heart's, white and grey

Shift Azizi, the loveless; for her in no world, there's a stay!

Isabel Ayesha Khalid

(46)

Counting the star's on night sky,

In misery and memories, sleep I

Watching me crying and longing by,

The stars keep praying, to Merciful Shy

Seeing Your hair flutter, diving in Your night eye

Heedlessly is passing my life; O come by!

Before in longings, my life to me, greets its bye

69

Isabel Ayesha Khalid

(47)

Someday, when my all petals are plucked

I will remain, the only perfume, burning in You

The only essence left in Muhammed's heart

An ashed heart, who no one knew

Azizi awaits for this day to come

Till then she's a love-struck slew

Isabel Ayesha Khalid

Isabel Ayesha Khalid

(48)

Under the moonlight, sit I, with love of mine

Vanished all stars, on earth the Sun arrived

Stars my lamp, delighted we sat, in songs and wine

What happened to me; I changed, my words begin
to rhyme

In autumn bloomed my flowers; stars begin to align

Delightfully You took my hand, O how You called
me mine!

Four moons You assigned to me, in my heart, You
left Your sign

Stood all before Azizi! Since her name You wrote in
Divine

72

(49)

Under the same moon sit I; to which my Love would sight

It fragrant's like him; it's as he's with me right,

Here, spreading his hair across black night

Shining at the moon; so I may stumble not, making all bright

Now, I do understand why to me, would talk long the night

And to me, why does the Moon bless a smile

The Charmer of mine has left; yet, to Him I sight

Neither could I embrace, nor could I, leave in demise

Azizi turned into a Lover! Azizi! O poor might

Taking a sickness, whose cure remained beyond death's might

73

Isabel Ayesha Khalid

(50)

A flower of the desert, sings a song

Neither to the Earth, nor the heavens, was it known

But to the One, whom her heart did belong

The stars fell, couldn't bare her song

The green grew yellow, the spring turned harrow

Her love to hear, her ache became to strong

Even did the Creator hide, and secretly passed a smile

Isabel under the setting star's is await

When will the Sun rise; when arrives her dawn

Isabel Ayesha Khalid

(51)

Some words are unsaid; so some words, say not

The song of heart is for barren; flood not tears,

For leading to Beloved, You'll find no boat

Some called Shura, the other's Ruth and what not

The name I craved to hear; oh how he forgot?

Neither I'm drowning in memories; nor like dead,
he lets me float

Never I'm silent, nor have the courage to talk

With a mere gaze, in love with him, I fought

Call me Azizi and complete me

Before in ein soaf, we both are lost

75

Isabel Ayesha Khalid

(52)

Where I spot affection, there spot I, reflection of
You

O how strange is this, my unrelated relation to You

I can't call You mine; yet, for my rights, I'm fighting
with You

Azizi's Muhammed since I became, there was no
You with me

Deprived of You, lonely; yet, in my reflection
appeared You

(53)

A tale of Dawn, the song of night became I

A veil of bride, to hide her bright face, became I

A wired dance, a heretic's write I became

The unwritten law, the secret right I became

Blasphemy shutting Your mouth, to sush you quite, I became

Quit your thoughts, say your Koran and fight

İt's silent candle, in night shining, that white, I became

77

Isabel Ayesha Khalid

(54)

I fumble name stained glass of Yours

As if it were Your hand, I'd hold

Like the water touching, kissing the shores

Like the dew from dawn, against petals of rose

Just like that, I did touch it, with name of Your

Like the helpless gaze of wild in love

As if from sight of mine, my Love may shove

And yet, it may never see before

Just like it, I gaze at name of Your

Forsaken or forsaking I do not know

I seem to forget You, yet I'm crying on name of Your

Isabel Ayesha Khalid

(55)

Lillie's, from the finest vineyards vine, for You I'll
bring

With strings of Your heart, on finest day, a song I'll
sing

My desires in blood wrapped, to You I'll gift, from
my heart, to You my king

And till death slips away, my life to You I'll bring as
spring

I will bring You dew of the dawn

And from night, I'll buy You tears to drown

For the contrast begins, between Your eyes

And Your sweet lies, in heart of days frown

Like Sun and Moon, we will fight

79

Isabel Ayesha Khalid

With You I'll die; without You I cannot smile

Even then we'll stand, after all side by side

Hearing tales of our love, told by the night

All these days, I'll preserve that melody for You

So on promised day, You may know, my tears are true

Can't be whole in the whole without You; to You on promised day I'll cling

As night lights every star, let's be like them, don't let us fling

Isabel Ayesha Khalid

(56)

Queen of desert sold out to the wind

The wind got reckless, it begin to spin

Hitting the tides of blue and high, in grim

Of desert's flower drew her blind

Selling her to eden, drifted away the wind

Like one Lilly amongst thorns, was left her, at their whim

O my poor Child! Called the fire within

From its kingdom, she was sold, in water to swim

A dry river and Rosy liver, she burnt within

Singing the song of desert, its flute and shofar

Abandoned by the One, sold away so far

But will return one day, with the first blow

In arms of night will shed tears so slow

Isabel Ayesha Khalid

The Last of Azizi

With crown of desert upon her head

Azizi will be home, a home near yet, so far

Isabel Ayesha Khalid

(58)

Twelve lamps yet, none is known

One of them, a flame, I did burn

Twelve tribes lost in thrive

Others to prove wrong, themselves right

Lost in the hue and dust, alas with no gust!

The lion of Ismael lost its light

The wingless begin to fly, the winged lost its flight

The rulers did now in rule, lose their delight

Devastated Azizi in wilderness loses her might

Is this the Ismael, who's the world's light?

83

Isabel Ayesha Khalid

(59)

Of the blind, how many tears, You'll shed?

For unseen beauty, how much blood You expect?

In my garden, seeing the Rosy red

Offended, he called it, his liver's blood

Witness to this suffering, Your mysterious love, did lead

To console the broken heart, arrived the man, who so much read,

Scripted love, to preach, Lover's glowing led?

It is kept from You, You foolish man, this isn't your stead!

To remove from Rose it's red, do You intend?

Leave Azizi, to her, You better forget!

A bird of flight, to scripted love, never she read!

Isabel Ayesha Khalid

Entered I the sea of love, yet is empty my boat?

Isabel Ayesha Khalid

(60)

Like the stars spread across the desert, my heart's
broken

Like the trackless dunes, under the Sun, I lost my
love's heedless token

From the seven skies the One who dived, locked in
cage, I'm that injured Falcon

Now that Your name doesn't glue my heart, Azizi's
become a mirror so broken

Isabel Ayesha Khalid

(61)

Whose beauty to blind, may bless a sight,

And casts to seeing, a blind's blight

To the same honey Liped, I give my heart

To the citrus, Who became a healing

To the yearning a death's cruel dealing

İf you fear, to You He'll frown

If you don't, He'll color you in brown

To the heart of Azizi His love did mark

I Spark in Him, and with Him I'm dark

87

Isabel Ayesha Khalid

(62)

Since when did Lilies look like Your hair?

And the Sun picture You, O the One who's fair?

Since when with the soft, gentle blows of breeze,

Your rosy breath, with me did You share?

Across the night sky, since when my Love,

I found it covered with Your nightshade hair?

Azizi merged in the beauty that You share

Knowing that she's Your one true heir

88

Isabel Ayesha Khalid

(63)

Tearing of heart, ripping of soul, how does it feel?

Unseasoned cries, smiles often lies, how do they heal?

Your simple lips trade with heaven's glimpse, is it even real?

And he said, he won from the One, although he did conceal

In His eyes let me dive, for seven skies flight, I do not keel

For beauty lies not in such a sky, where all others fly

To me is One sky, concealed in Your eyes, where to my self I see

Heaven I do not need, all I desire, within me, Your breath to feel

89

Perhaps foolish I am, folly is better than,

Staying in follies paradise, forsaking my love, my

glee

90

Isabel Ayesha Khalid

(65)

To my words, Your blind eyes, how could see?

During love's storms You stayed in a lee

Now to my words, You think You'll perceive?

Advice not thee, suggesting words for me!

I am a drop that contains a sea

The sea of words never known to thee

For a lover like me, a lover, you could never be!

Isabel Ayesha Khalid

(66)

In my heart trapped a silent sadness

Like crimson of eve, decorated in me

A silent yet pleasant, my mystery sadness

Said I, 'I know not, of what's my madness'

Cry in tears then I, praying for thee

From me, kept I my secret, my pleasant shyness

...

92

(67)

On his chest, when I lay

Like a cloud soaring in heaven's bay

İn greed of heaven, left you İ, one day

But when shifted I, in heaven to stay

Burnt I in hell, burnt, missing your sway!

So what is heaven, what do You say?

To me, remained You, my holy way

To God I begged, I begged, died I

'To me You exile, exile' I pray!

To me You stayed heaven, your love my fay

93

Isabel Ayesha Khalid

(68)

My beloved is gone, you said, 'He was never Your'

Sickened am I, with no disease, with no cure

Drowned I, in seas of love, with no water, with no
shore

In thirst died I, overflowing with water, in between
a bore

Yes! Sickened am I, with no symptoms, with no cure

Am I in my mind, asked He, am I sure?

Although was He my heart, He is the One, who cast
the door,

Open to me, and of love, made me a drawer

Then drawed the One, never existed who, and made
me crawl

94

Isabel Ayesha Khalid

And above the skies to me gave flights, and again made me fall

Like a child in search of milk, on floor he made me roll

And a dying bird in fire, like fish out of water, to me he trawl

And now is surprised He, why I brawl?

Yes I'm sick, sick am I, there's no cure

And mocked me silently, silently did, the ones my sincere

Calling me innocent, an innocent affair

İt did break my heart, tore my flesh and now they stare?

What's wrong with her, the one in all who's fair?

İs there no shame, no shame in you, you share?

Upon my pain, to me, how do you glare?

95

Isabel Ayesha Khalid

You let me, a mirror fall into countless pieces and snare

To me before, you never warned, I might be spared!

Yes again my sincere do gather! My sincerest dear

You kept me dear, but to warm, you never could dare

To spice my pain, once again, now you're here

In fantasy to me you did keep, is that even fare?

That fantasy that's now my reality

Although she's dead, I do feel Azizi in me, here and there

Not as a spring but a deadly news she brings

Neither in fact nor in fantasy, a lie,

A bird am I, a bird who lost her wings!

Isabel Ayesha Khalid

(69)

Shall I, across my face, let it flow?

Or perhaps calling it phase, say it no?

Calling it evidence of love, in it I row?

Perhaps being patient, I let it, not go?

Should I keep you in eye, O tear for my dear?

Preserve you, shall I, or with You I go?

Causing redness in my eyes, wearing a bloody rose

Seeing the rose, turned away I, from Him

Offended, calling it, of my liver a rosy glow

And perhaps of my pain, He made a show!

You think it's funny? From my livers roses you grow?

You are my God, my dear or to me, my foe?

97

Isabel Ayesha Khalid

Can't decide I, can't take it anymore!

Through the eve's of sky, through the perfect sigh,

Offend me not, offend me not anymore!

Isabel Ayesha Khalid

(70)

In love a bittersweet game, a hide and seek I play

Longing for Your warmth, hiding under winter's sway

Afraid to see You, I shut eyes, then cry to see Your face

What a fool I am? What strange game I play!

For He was once mine and still he remains

First would I hide; for the both roles, now I'm the only player!

Like the dawning Sun He did set, He never rose again

Like the Rose in Autumn He slept, leaving His garden vain

Swept He across my heart's field

99

Isabel Ayesha Khalid

Yet slept I, when His scent crossed near

For afraid was I, to miss Him and not find Him here!

Longed to hear from Him, yet deafen to hear his name

Called Him loud but hid, before he called my name

Oh what state am I in, a state of shame!

Here I call to be with Him, and flee again

But me, whom can I blame?

A lonely Lover became I, finding and seeking His fame

The only player in hide and seek game!

I am the center of the world's deride

For a sane like me, fell for some mystery eyes

Come so I may show them, come and do not hide

The eyes, when seen by a living, he died

Gave life to the dead, whom life defied

And to my seeing eyes, who did blind

To my blind foe, the one who eyed

O come my lovely eyed! O come and do not hide!

In longings to see You, day and night I cried

A mystery ocean of tears before me,

It drowns me in and yet remains all dried

Maybe so is my love for You, I dive in You,

I'm all in You, but thirst like I never dived

101

O how to me, Your raven hair would seem?

Spread across the night-shade sky

To me they became a guide

İn Your curls my heart was fully tied

My soul in You was fully dyed

Yet, I and You are unrecognizable

İ tried we may look alike, I tried but didn't fruit my stride

You were my sight, but You, my seeings never defined

O Your fragrant hair, what a perfume they have?

What essence it has, confide in me, do not hide!

Shall I call it the musk of dawn, or scent of night-sky?

Do they smell like rose, or rosy is pretty dry?

102

Isabel Ayesha Khalid

Or maybe something that nothing may define

Perhaps that's why, God concealed it fine!

For I am a jealous God, he would say once

Now that i became Yours, people to me defied?

O come my mystery eyed,

O come the one, upon whom its creator spied

Intensely for You, day and night I cried

I cried a drowning lake, and yet is dried

(72)

What voice is this, calling me, chanting my soul?

How loud it is, deafs me to all, swallowing me whole!

Colder than snow, lighter than straw, is this Your call?

For sake of hearing from You, an endless track, I begin to stroll

Rising above sky, in longings I fall

To hear one last time, You call, that's all!

Isabel Ayesha Khalid

(73)

The heaven's and Earth merged in my grief, O
come!

For the One, beautiful than all, the Sun the moon,

The heavenly stars, with me begin to gloom, O
come!

Like eve Sun melting in the ocean's bay, this noon

İn Your grief my heart did melt, Oh no relief, O
come!

İf I mean something, any worth I reap O love,

İn Your sight, do not hide, don't leave, O come!

Silently in Your room I enter and leave

I snoop to hear Your voice, like a thief, O come

Say I'm not forsaken, say come my love!

Even if You won't, I'll still believe, O come!

Isabel Ayesha Khalid

That from Your departure, to me You'll grant a
release, O come!

O love, do me a favor and come by

Before I stand lonely, like the morning sky

Now come, O come and be not shy

Come before my soul to me does deny

O come dear one, O do come by!

So someday, when I see the rising Sun

It won't be cold, for I would see it with You

And when I see the night moon, so full

It won't be strange, for You'll complete me so true

So come to me my love, come to me

O the one, the only, whom my heart knew

106

Isabel Ayesha Khalid

(74)

Still like my dreams, in arms of reckless winds,
stand I

In embrace of spring-full life, a continuous death I
die

For You're not here, never were You, here by

In all to You I see, although never seen by my pity
eye

Every passing wind to me does blame, for saying
You bye

Although it's You who left, leaving me here in
world's deserted isle

It's whispering to me, whispering again that I'm the
shy!

Oh what a test it is, is it the wind or my conscious'
sigh?

107

Isabel Ayesha Khalid

İt's raining and sit I, under the open sky

Seeing the drops kissing the Earth goodbye

How fleeting the moment is, how gentle the kiss?

İt dances over the ground but doesn't stay by

But never did get a moment with You, oh never did I

*As short as the dancing drop that upon the ground
once did lay*

*What if I get that moment with You, and You come
by*

*Shortest like the dancing drop, longest like the
endless sky*

O what could we have done! O what I could desire?

Perhaps the rising Sun with You I'd see?

What's cold, to me warm forever it'd seem

108

Isabel Ayesha Khalid

For without You, Sun never rose for me

O the Moon, what if the full moon we'd see

For it's to me always a divided seed

Or maybe into Your eyes I'd dive

For mine remains a thirsty sea

Waiting for You, for Beloved to see

Although an impossible to me it seems

Or perhaps Your sound, a melody I'd hear

Would it smell like embers so clear

For I'm deaf, except You I'd never hear

Although screams the world, but İt's a lonely year

Like the dancing drop against the floor

İ wish to meet at least once more

109

Isabel Ayesha Khalid

The Last of Azizi

You seem familiar yet I'd never known

I know Your scent, though Your flower I'd never
sown

Your voice, Oh how familiar to me

I'd never heard, yet it echo's in me

Let's meet again just once again

Like the dancing drop, bless me Your fame...

Isabel Ayesha Khalid

(75)

Tonight in Your arms, to my self I saw; wake me
not!

Tearing heart and pouring eyes await; wake me
not!

For desert found her rain, in pain return her not;
wake me not!

A Jasmine I bloom with no rose, this prose I present
to You; wake me not!

Let the night stay night for me, Sun for me never
rose; wake me not!

A rose in my garden blooms, with bounty and
perfumes; wake me not!

Now grave to Azizi became heavens and Earth her
hell,

Let her sleep in wild, with breath of him so mild;
wake me not!

111

Isabel Ayesha Khalid

Begged I, don't kill the dead!

Isabel Ayesha Khalid

(76)

Midst of galaxy travelled I, between me, no star
does float

Entered I the home of Beloved, for him a poem I
wrote

My pillow next to him, was nothing but a deathly
moat

During the blizzard rose my heart's burning smoke

That kept Him warm and save from cold

To Him, even my suffering stayed so devote

After miles found I that full gathering, and yet there
You're not?

For how on this Earth so whole, could I stay whole?

For from me You slipped away, through I silent
hole!

113

Isabel Ayesha Khalid

*In empty boat, in time forsaken, lonely Azizi does
float*

*With empty tales of headless journey, with nothing
to boast*

Isabel Ayesha Khalid

The Last of Azizi

Isabel Ayesha Khalid

(77)

Out of my flesh, I'll sew a cloak for You

From my soul, I'll bloom a rose so true

To keep You warm, I'll present my heart's burning
stew

Tisk, You will leave! And move with another crew!

And if ever You cry, or loose in autumn's hue

Pluck out my petal, sniff deep in my fragrance for
You

Yet again You shall leave, with another, You may
crew

In the middle of desert, if You loose

Smile at other, out of anguish, spring's of water I'll
flow

Quench Your thirst, with another walk through

116

Isabel Ayesha Khalid

Causing You relief, would end my rue

(78)

The One who's warmth of wheaty cheeks,

Art of blush, taught sky of eve's

And when the Sun was at a hush

With fragrant hair, Who covers sky that seeks,

And for the autumn's await mush

Who's smile became a rosy lush

I am the fish of Lover's sea

İf you taste, you may reek

For Love is kindled in firey geek

Against such Love, how can I leap?

Lest Sun is torn away, the stars asleep,

117

Isabel Ayesha Khalid

Who cloud cause an eve, a blush, who could teach?

For night's silent love who could speak?

For me new dawn, without Him, how could be?

For Moon never replaced the Sun

Without Your smile, in water I'd never run

You ask to forget Him, is it your sum?

Has a boat sailed without a Sea?

Did flower's bloom without their Seed?

Does the clam calm without her Bead?

How queer without Him, is for me to think?

For all night is colorless, without Your hair

The eve is dark, deprived of seeing You fair,

Isabel Ayesha Khalid

The fish may die, without their Layer

So how come I breathe, without Him near?

For Azizi without her Sun, a dawn could never come

Return, for to Muhammad I'll never shun...!

Yes the Sun is torn away, the stars asleep

Without You my love, my breath in me, how could I keep?

Without You pump Your love in me, how could, my heart beat?

Yes the Sun is torn away, the stars asleep!

Yet I couldn't drift away, for You I weep

Lost in mellows of wilderness, I am that sheep

Without the hand of Muhammad, into hell, who could slip

119

Isabel Ayesha Khalid

The Last of Azizi

Yes the Sun is torn away, the stars asleep!

Yet another than You, offered to me, I cannot keep

Without the blush in eve, I'd never see

In nights without Your hair I'd never sleep

All that slept was the flesh, the soul with thee

Even if tears the Sun, my every tear to You will keep,

In safe memories, in streams flooding off from me

Azizi to You will keep dear, without You, is no me!

Although the Sun's torn apart, the stars asleep!

Isabel Ayesha Khalid

THE TURKIC WORLD

121

The Last of Azizi

Poetic prose:

Qoy könlüm qoparın; çün məndən qoparıldığı sən
gibi

Let me rip out my heart; for You were ripped away,
just like that, from me

Qoy gözlüm görməsin; çün gülüşün sən, görmürəm
mən kor kimi

Let my eyes not see; for You smiling, I cannot see,
like a blind I be!

Qoy qulaqlarım eşitməmək; eşitməkdən başqa ne
dəymək ki?

Let my ears to hear not! For other than You, what's
hearing?

Dilbər bir can bizi! Sənsiz mən cansız cismi; Ah
Səbrimi qədərmi?

Isabel Ayesha Khalid

O Charmer of Me! We are one soul, İ and thee!
Without You, I am a dead body; Alas! How much
patience You'll squeeze of me?

Tüh! Eşqimi qəbrəmi oldu; qəlbimi oldu əzabımı

Alas! Became my Beloved, grave of me; heart of
mine, my torture became!

Nəsimidən öyrənin Əzizi! Mən dünyamı itirəndə, ne
öyrənmək?

Learn from Your Nesimi, Aziz! When I lose my
world, to me now, what's meant to learn?

Isabel Ayesha Khalid

Sənsız dünya ey yar, başqa dünya ey yar istəməm

Ne var xətaya? ey yar sənsız bahar ne var, istəməm

Sənsız canım bimar, arzü hiç, səmsız ah səvar, hoş
istəməm

Günəşsız qəmli qəmgin ay mən Əzizi, başqa
Muhammad sevdar istəməm

Şarap nedir kim ben O Saqi kimdir?

Şeriat nedir ey Şair, her din siri vardir

Ruhdir gercek, kim ruhim; ney bedendir?

Ney kelime, ney kader ve beyandir?

Dünya acayip zindan; farkı kışın yazdan nedir?

Ve farkı yağmurun gözyaşımdan ne vardir?

Kim aşik ve maşüq, ney aşqdir?

Miskin Azizi! ol aşk ve ruh Saqidir

Kokusuz gül nedir

Aşksız gönül nedir

Ruhsuz beden nedir

Sözsüz derviş gider

Tüh! Bülbül bahçesi biter

Isısız ateş gibidir,

Susuz su Kimidir

Görmeyen gözler, gibidir

Tüh! Leylasız Mecnu

Sözsüz derviş gider

Güneşsiz ay nedir

Muhammedsiz Azizi nedir

Tüh! Aşksız şair gider

Isabel Ayesha Khalid

*Aşk oyununda kazanan kaybeder, kaybeden
kaybeder*

*Parlamaz ben ay gibi, hilal kaybeder, kazanan
dolunay benden kaybeder*

Öfkeli bir cahil gibi, ben kaybettim bana benden

Yazık Azizi sultan olmak fakir gibi yaşdım

127

The Last of Azizi

Ey aşkım! Ey canım benim!

Yüreğimi yerle bir ettin

Yalnızca benim, yalnızca benim olunca

Bu gözler mi suçlu bu aşka düşmemde,

Sana tutkun olmamda, sonsuz kayboluşumda,

Dünyayı kör edip sadece seni görmemde

Ey gözler, okyanustan da derin sular

Aşkınla beni susuzlukla kavuruyorsun

Peki saçların, ey saçların aşkım?

Kokuların solgunları bile utandırır, ey saçların
aşkım

Sarışın bu kıvrımlarda kaybolup gidiyorum

Güneşin şarkısını söyleyen gece gibi

Ey senin için esir düştüğüm nedir?

Belki de sesindir, ey sesin aşkım

Isabel Ayesha Khalid

Baldan daha tatlı, tüm acıları savuran

Ey aşkım, her ne olursa olsun tamamen seninim

Yalnızca benim olduğunu söylemek, ne büyük bir mutluluk

Bu gözler, uçsuz bucaksız bir okyanus, sadece benim

Bu saçlar, güneşten daha parlak, sadece benim

Bu ses, balın ötesinde tatlı, sadece benim

Isabel Ayesha Khalid

Gel ey sevgili, gör aşkıma olan divaneyim

Bak ne kadar çılgınca sana olan aşkım

Neden bu denli tutkunum sana, anlam veremem

Beynimdeki bu ateşi nasıl da söndüremem

Mavi gözlerinle başladı bu büyülü yolculuk

Sürüklendim derin sularına, aşkınla doldum, dolup taştım

Gözlerin okyanus mavisi, gönlümde yankılanır

Kayboldum o güzellikte, aşkınla tutkuya dönüşür

Bir bakışınla alev aldım, yandım ateşinle

Gözlerin beni sarıp sarmaladı, aşkla besledi içimdeki ateşi

Isabel Ayesha Khalid

Altın saçların güneş gibi parlar, ışıldar

Kokuların eser etrafa, kor gibi yanar, büyüler

Sana ait olmanın gururu içindeyim, benimsin sadece

Kimselere ait değilsin, gururla söylerim, benim sevgilim, eşimsin sadece

Gel ey sevgili, gel, kalbim seni bekler

Bu aşkımı anlatsam da anlamazlar, sadece sen hisset, sen bilirsin, sen eşsizlersin

131

Isabel Ayesha Khalid

The Last of Azizi

Kimin bu sesi, ruhumu çağıran,

Sesin kudreti, yüreğimi dağlayan.

Kara kıştan soğuk, saman hafifliğiyle,

İçimi kemiren, sarsan bu çağrıyı duyan.

Kendini gösteren, bir hayal mi bu yoksa?

Izabel, sesin mi, yoksa rüyamın toplasa?

Ulaşmak için sana, bitmek bilmeyen bir yola,

Adımlarım düşüyor, yükseliyorum buluta.

Gökyüzünde yükselirken, hasretle iniyorum,

Tek bir kez daha duymak için çağrını, içim yanıyor.

Izabel, ismimi an, son bir defa daha,

Bensizliğin ağırlığına son ver, sesinle yakınlaşayım

sana.

Isabel Ayesha Khalid

Translation

Whose voice is this that summons my soul's deep abyss,

With its resounding might, piercing my heart's core amiss.

Colder than winter's embrace, lighter than straw's bliss,

This haunting call within, consuming, shaking, I reminisce.

Does it reveal a fleeting dream or a reality grand?

Isabel, is it Your voice or a conjuring of my command?

On an endless path, reaching out to You, hand in hand,

My steps falter, ascending towards clouds, unplanned.

133

As I rise above the heavens, with yearning I descend,

Craving to hear Your call again, my soul ablaze, it transcends.

Isabel, utter my name, one final time, before this chapter ends,

Relieve the weight of solitude, let our voices entwine, as fate amends.

Isabel Ayesha Khalid

www.ingramcontent.com/pod-product-compliance
Lightning Source LLC
Chambersburg PA
CBHW062314290526
45794CB00005B/1800